W9-CNO-398

PowerKiDS Readers
THE UNIVERSE

THE SUN

Elisa Peters

PowerKiDS press™

New York

Published in 2013 by The Rosen Publishing Group, Inc.
29 East 21st Street, New York, NY 10010

First Edition

Editor: Amelie von Zumbusch
Book Design: Kate Laczynski

Photo Credits: Cover Frank Zullo/Photo Researchers/Getty Images; pp. 4, 6, 8, 10, 12, 14, 18, 20, 22, 24 (earth, sun, plants) Shutterstock.com; p. 16 Science Source/Photo Researchers/Getty Images.

Library of Congress Cataloging-in-Publication Data

Peters, Elisa.
    The sun / by Elisa Peters. — 1st ed.
        p. cm. — (Powerkids readers: the universe)
    Includes index.
    ISBN 978-1-4488-7385-2 (library binding) — ISBN 978-1-4488-7465-1 (pbk.) —
ISBN 978-1-4488-7537-5 (6-pack)
    1. Sun—Juvenile literature. I. Title.
    QB521.5.P47 2013
    523.7—dc23
                                            2011043723

Manufactured in the United States of America

CPSIA Compliance Information: Batch #CS12PK: For Further Information contact Rosen Publishing, New York, New York at 1-800-237-9932

CONTENTS

The Sun   5

So Hot!   15

Keeping Earth Warm   21

Words to Know   24

Index   24

Websites   24

Earth circles the **Sun**.

6

The Sun is a star.

8

It is made of gas.

10

It always sets in the west.

Eight **planets** circle the Sun.

14

The Sun is hot.

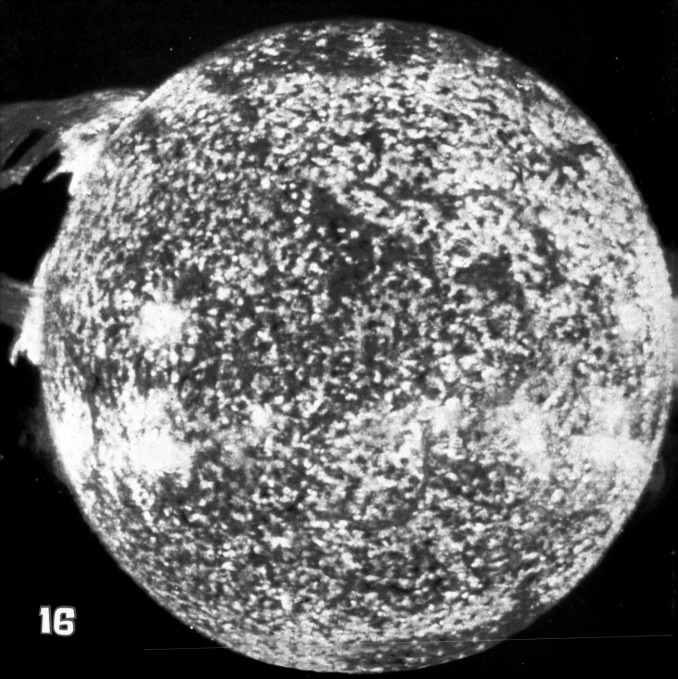

It is hottest in the middle.

18

It is 4.6 billion years old.

It keeps Earth warm.

Plants need its light to grow.

WORDS TO KNOW

planet

plants

Sun

INDEX

E
Earth, 5, 21

G
gas, 9

L
light, 23

P
plants, 23

WEBSITES

Due to the changing nature of Internet links, PowerKids Press has developed an online list of Web sites related to the subject of this book. This site is updated regularly. Please use this link to access the list:
www.powerkidslinks.com/pkrtu/sun/